THE TIMES

odd jobs

~~Unusual~~ ways to earn a living

Simon Kent

KOGAN PAGE

First published in 2000
Reprinted 2000

Kogan Page Limited
120 Pentonville Road
London N1 9JN

The views expressed in this book are the views of the author, and are not necessarily the same as those of Times Newspapers Ltd.

British Library Cataloguing in Publication Data

A CIP record for this book is available from the British Library.

ISBN 0 7494 3249 7

Typeset by Saxon Graphics Ltd, Derby
Printed and bound in Great Britain by Clays Ltd, St Ives plc

Contents

Contents

And So
To Work

Warning! This is not a careers book. This book will not tell you what to do with the rest of your life and at no point will it tell you how to write a good CV.

However, this book *will* help you find a fun, off-the-wall job and, moreover, a job that you want to do. Steering clear of Careers Centre pamphlets, avoiding Job Centre notice boards and careers fairs, it takes a less-beaten track, heading for out of the way places, territories you may have thought of only in passing and some you may never have considered.

While this book clearly features certain jobs and roles you may want to pursue, the search does not end there. Each section begins with an introductory piece that covers certain aspects of the job market and suggests ways into the workplace. Even the job descriptions themselves are not always limited to one single activity, exploring instead related possibilities and encouraging you to think laterally about what you can do.

If you have an interest, a hobby, an obsession or a passion for something, this book can help you turn that positive energy into a livelihood. If you can name what you want to do for a living but everyone tells you to be realistic or says, 'No one will pay you to do that!', this book will put you on the right track to realizing your goal.

Too good to be true? Not really! Today's workplace is an incredibly diverse and fast-moving place. There is always a place for the entrepreneur – the person who spots a new opportunity and has the determination to follow it through. Imagination, energy and enthusiasm are prized above academic achievement, company loyalty and kowtowing to corporate structures. In this way, the Internet has not only introduced a whole new media and business area in which people can work, it has brought together formerly disparate individuals, creating new marketing opportunities and causing traditional business to re-invent itself. Add to this an increase in leisure time and leisure spend for many people, and what do you get? A whole pile of *odd jobs*.

In researching this book, I found that many people involved in these jobs did not perceive their work to be outlandish. It was also clear that very often there were elements of the work that were run of the mill and amounted to everyday basic grind, which results in long hours to be worked and not enough money in the pay packet. However, what makes these jobs special is that they tap into areas of workers' personalities – parts of their lives that would be important even if they weren't doing this job for a living. Therefore, the motivation they experience is not connected to monetary recognition or the conventional trappings of status, but to something much more powerful – something that means the hours, the hard work and the grind is more than worth it.

The trick to finding this kind of work is to think laterally. Burn the rule books and don't take 'no' for an answer! Think about what you want to do, what you can do and the context in which you can do it. Think about the people who might pay you to do it and those you might need to help you in that position. Think of yourself as fitting in to a supply and demand chain: who are the customers who will want your service or product, and who are the suppliers who can give you the raw materials? How will what you do add value to your customers' lives?

Frequently, these jobs require self-employment or even the establishment of a new business. This demands a whole new set of skills and self-discipline from you in order to work alone, to attract customers and ensure the business survives. It is difficult but extremely rewarding work, and it can mean going to work has simply become a way of being paid to play.

Technology has radically changed the world of work, and it has also altered the game of job hunting. The amount of information now accessible through the World Wide Web is inconceivable. For the job seeker, or anyone who wants to know more about one particular area of work, a first step is to find a good search engine and type in a few key words. The results could well be life changing.

Jobbing it for enjoyment

Work does not need to be a hardship. In fact, work can be fun! If you play your cards right, you may never have a single day's work that isn't exciting, fulfilling and satisfying. With a little imagination and a lot of enthusiasm, you can line up a whole range of perfect jobs – activities you enjoy so much that the pay packet is simply the icing on the cake.

Having spent so many years in the education system, you may feel it's time to prove your skills in the real world and show what you really can do. But is this possible by immediately finding a life-long employer who wants you to contribute to their firm in their way? Having spent so long gaining knowledge and honing your skills, do you really want to take a position that may only exercise you in a few of these areas? Why should work be a place where you leave your imagination behind, or even your personality? Checking in for a day's work should not mean clicking in to the same old routine, it should mean triggering your motivation and excitement.

Right now you have the ideal opportunity to experiment in the workplace – to find different things to do, take on new challenges and play a wide variety of roles. You can take jobs simply because you like the look of them. You can take seasonal work to suit your lifestyle: outdoor or travel-related work during the summer, indoor work during the winter. You can try out a physically demanding job to see whether you are suited to it, and then try something more technical or office-based so that you are able to compare the two. You do not need to commit yourself to a long-term contract but can determine for yourself how long you want to stay with each employer. After the prescriptive lifestyle of full-time education, *you* are now in charge of what you do – and no one else.

Full-time employment takes up a lot of time – about a third of your life will be spent working. And that will still affect the other two thirds – and not just by giving you the means with which you can live. It may demand overtime and fill your head with problems and issues you'd rather not think about on your days off. It may determine your leisure time, how you dress and how you speak. When you meet other people, your job will be one of the primary methods by which they will identify you. Trying out a range of jobs will give you an insight into all of these identities to find the one that suits you best.

Certainly you will need to work to earn money in order to be able to live but work should not be a purely financial transaction. Work should give you a full range of life experiences, such as working with different people and initiating and completing your own projects – thrills and spills in equal measure. At this early stage in your career you are perfectly placed to demand those experiences from your working life. A few years down the line, your priorities and responsibilities may have changed, but as a newly-qualified entrant to the job market the world is your playground.

There have never been more ways of tracking down fun, interesting and bizarre things to do for a living than there are today. The communications revolution has made the world a smaller place and established all kinds of links between people and organizations that simply did not exist before. The Internet can put you in touch with people from all over the world, people who can offer advice and opportunities, and people who will be more than happy to be your future customers. Think globally in your search for work. You may not fancy working the photocopier in an office in your local town, but what if, as soon as you have finished, you could walk out into the sunshine and relax on Bondi Beach?

Prioritize your job search according to what you want to do, as much as by what you are qualified to do. Volunteer your services wherever practical or necessary and work for the experience you will gain. Find people you want to work with rather than having your social circle forced upon you through work colleagues. Find a job that identifies you as an individual, and highlights your imagination and personality.

So go ahead: pick up the phone and dial the company who has the job you've always wondered about. Find out what skills you need to be a roller skating waiter or waitress in a New York café. Surf the Web and discover what opportunities there are for you as a fire-eating minstrel in Australia. And most of all, work hard and work fun.

Getting Technical

There is little doubt that the PC and the Internet together offer the greatest opportunity for work and careers than practically anything else. Demand for Internet skills already outstrips supply – a situation which is likely to remain constant well into the future. Moreover, the proliferation of PCs in every workplace means applicants for all kinds of jobs will be more employable if they can show computer skills. Therefore, the good news is that you do not need to be a college graduate in computer science to secure a place in one of the new technology companies. Provided you can show evidence of the right skills you can be self-taught – all you need to do is offer employers some great ideas and prove that you can carry out the work they want you to do.

This aspect of the industry is likely to change in the future. At the moment the vast majority of employees in Internet companies have transferred from more traditional industries. As time goes by there will be workers who have spent their whole careers in the industry and it will be these people who reap the rewards in the job market. Newcomers to the industry will then have to offer specific Internet or technology-related qualifications in order to compete.

Throughout the Internet and games market the workplace appears to be split between 'techies' and 'creatives' – those who can program and those who can come up with ideas on what should appear on Web pages and so on. While you will find yourself working in one or the other of these areas, the more understanding of both these skills you can offer, the higher your value will be in the job market.

Web page designer

As the Internet is recognized as a business tool, more and more organizations are looking to this medium to carry advertisements, contact details and company information. It has been said that any company which does not have an Internet presence in three years time will no longer be in business. Currently, good Web designers are at a premium and can charge great sums of money for doing what is, in truth, simple programming work.

Many of today's Web page designers have advertising or marketing backgrounds but as time goes by the pure Web page designer will emerge – people who have worked solely with the Internet as their medium and therefore understand completely what it can do. Today it is still possible to get a job with a Web design agency on the evidence of ability rather than academic qualifications. If you have created your own sophisticated Web page, you may be able to convince employers that you are what they need.

The first stage of the work is to pitch ideas for the Web pages to clients. Unlike traditional advertising media – newspapers and TV – Web pages can be updated instantly and the technology is advancing at such a speed that what is possible today is likely to be old hat by next week. Therefore, when presenting a pitch, it is necessary to be clear about exactly what clients are going to get for their money. If other ideas emerge while working on that page, they should be treated under a separate project. Without this kind of arrangement, designers can find they have worked for many months on a single Web page and received insufficient remuneration.

Obviously, the best Web pages are those that attract large numbers of visitors and keep them there for a long time. This can be done using different techniques – offering interactive features on the site or designing the site to provide specific information for visitors.

There are no standards to the structure or operation of Web design companies, so designers may find themselves working in all sorts of situations – in teams, alone, on long-term projects or small parts of other projects. Designers need to use a wide range of programming languages in order to carry out different tasks on the Web page. The industry has a young and mobile workforce who move from company to company easily, attracted by the variety and type of work on offer as much as by remuneration.

 Highs: Building innovative sites and breaking new ground in design.

 Lows: Matching the ideas for Web pages with what is practically possible.

Computer game designer and builder

Home entertainment has become big business as games consoles now bring arcade style amusements into the living-room. The industry needs both creative and technical people to imagine and drive the games forward. As the industry has developed, there has been a shift in entrance requirements with increased preferences for high academic achievers. However, there is still room for the maverick – the genius who has been programming the home computer for years and knows every game inside out.

The studios where the games are created employ a hierarchy of workers devoted to specific game projects. The creative director oversees the entire process of putting the game together from the initial idea for the game through to the final appearance of characters and background, sound effects and special effects used in the game. Alongside the director is the producer whose job it is to ensure the project is brought in on schedule in terms of money and time. Beneath these two are a team of workers ranging from concept artists, who provide the first visual input into a game, through to the programmers who make the game work and even musicians who write and record the necessary background music and any incidental sound effects. Again, there is frequently compromise in developing a game as the vision of the game's designers proves difficult for the programmers to realize.

One of the more junior jobs a technical worker can expect to take on is as a level mapper. In this role programmers map out the area in which the game is played – they assign certain qualities to the 3-D space ensuring that characters cannot walk through walls but can open doors and blow up other items. In this way games players will not find suddenly that they are able to move through walls or travel outside the game.

All workers in the industry, whether designing or programming the intricacies of the game, must have a sound knowledge of the computer games market.

Highs: Creating new games that can have thousands of people hooked to their games modules.

 Lows: Working to deadlines on this kind of project can be stressful and sometimes the work involves dealing with problems more than it involves being creative.

Computer games tester

No new computer game is released until it has been rigorously tested by professional game players. For this reason, game design studios employ devoted players to test the game thoroughly – trying every part of the game to ensure it works properly and will not crash in spite of everything a player might do during the course of playing. This means playing a game over and over for days at a time, sometimes video-taping the game as it is played in order to capture bugs in the programming as they happen.

Quality Assurance (QA) staff carry out this analysis. They will provide feedback on the design of the game, on features such as how easy it is to move through each level to complete the game and how easy the controls are to understand and operate. Aside from playing games, QA staff need to be good communicators, able to explain problems precisely and to provide useful feedback for the programmers or game designers. QA staff are rarely employed on a full-time or even on a regular basis they are not required by a games company until the product is almost ready for release and this can be between six and eight months from the inception of the game. However, it is possible to find work moving around the industry – playing games for different manufacturers and making a living that way.

A knowledge of programming skills can be useful for QA employees so they can suggest solutions to any glitches they encounter, but certainly the most important requirement is a complete and all-encompassing knowledge of the games market. If QA players have played similar games, they will be able to feed back on how the new product measures up. There may be certain features or something about the way a games console is used that the new game can incorporate. They can also tell the designers how addictive the game is – a quality that the designers and programmers themselves may find difficult to assess since they have worked on the game for so long.

 Highs: You get to play games all day – long before anyone else gets to buy them in the shops.

 Lows: Playing the same game day in, day out for weeks at a time can get tedious.

Web site games programmer

There are many new companies who generate revenue from Internet activity. These companies make their money by selling advertising space on the Web or by charging their visitors, either directly or through phone connection charges. In order to ensure advertisers want to buy space and visitors stay online to view the adverts, the Web company must create a high standard of content that will attract visitors and keep them coming back to the site. If a Web provider can show that a large amount of traffic crosses their site, they will be able to sell advertising space at a higher price than a site that has a low volume of traffic. One way of doing this is to offer a range of entertainment products for visitors to try out, such as games and other interactive services.

Due to the current nature of Internet browsers, the games featured on many Web sites are limited to using the 'point and click' mouse or simple typing functions. This means the games are kept to a simple level, for example, versions of games such as Hangman or Pontoon. However, there is always room for imagination. One site developed a very popular game called 'Slap a Spice' which combined the elements of a fairground sideshow game with the general annoyance directed towards the Spice Girls.

Designing a game and deciding its functions are usually a matter of teamwork but once the details are set, creating the program becomes a technical exercise using the most appropriate programming language, which is often Visual Basic. Translating the idea into an actual program can lead to some compromises when features identified at the design stage prove too difficult to program.

Web pages might also include other features which need to be designed and programmed. These may be in the form of greetings cards that can be sent by email users to their friends or virtual pets that can be downloaded. Depending on the size of the company, the programmer may work within a small team or on their own. However, in most cases, there will be teamwork and flexibility required since the content of a Web page changes rapidly according to new technology and the changing expectations of visitors.

 Highs: Working around problems and discovering how to program certain features.

 Lows: Long hours.

Technical support

Every day technology finds a new function in the workplace or in the home and every day new users discover the delights of having a printer that does not talk to their computer or a program that refuses to do what it is told or what it is meant to do. Guiding people in the proper use of their new technology does not require a high degree of information technology (IT) knowledge and can be the gateway to a lucrative career in the technology industry.

Dedicated telephone call centres have been set up to provide 24-hours-a-day support to technology users from all areas of home and work life. These centres are scattered all over the country and since you receive full training in computers before you start work, they can give you the chance to become a computer boffin and help other people work their technology at the same time.

Armed with a phone headset and a computer display giving details of the caller and the specific model and type of technology the caller is using, you can help customers through difficult procedures or diagnose problems by running through a checklist to detect where problems might have occurred.

Helpdesks are run to cover manufacturers' needs rather than any specific organizations so it is possible you will be helping an office employer one minute, a home user the next. In each case you need patience, a good phone manner and strong interpersonal skills to find out what the problem is and to encourage them to take the right action to solve that problem.

Many call centres put their staff on training and development programmes that provide recognized qualifications. At the lower end of the scale, the European Computer Driving Licence demonstrates the holder knows the basics of how a computer works and how to operate one. There are NVQs and the very well-regarded Microsoft qualifications that demonstrate the holder has passed certain standards for dealing with Microsoft technology. These latter qualifications are popular throughout the new industry and can lead to bigger and better jobs.

 Highs: Helping diverse customers to use their IT in effective ways.

Lows: Calls can be repetitive.

Environmental tester

This technical role occurs towards the final stages of the design process in many manufacturing businesses. Essentially, it is the environmental tester's duty to ensure a product is up to the job for which it has been created. Testers are used to make sure mobile phones can withstand the abuse their owners are likely to inflict on them during everyday use. They are used to show that street lighting can still operate in spite of the rigours of the British weather. They even simulate conditions in space to ensure satellites will operate having endured the experience of being blasted out of the earth's atmosphere on top of a rocket.

It is a very creative role in which technicians carefully study the conditions that the product will be subject to and design suitable experiments to simulate those effects. They then subject the product to those tests – this may be a prototype or the actual equipment itself. Street lighting must still be able to operate regardless of rain, wind and extremes of temperature. The testers will therefore set up the light inside a wind tunnel and see what happens when they subject it to strong winds over a certain period of time. They may immerse the lighting shield in water to check for leaks. They will also measure the light levels coming off the fitting and make sure this is suitable for its intended job.

By looking at the way mobile phones are treated – left inside cars, falling out of pockets and so on – testers can devise comparable temperature tests and drop tests. For the latter, every phone tested is dropped on to concrete in order to measure how robust the unit is. Testing technology for use in space holds particular challenges and so environmental testers in this field use vacuum chambers and vibrating machines to simulate conditions during the launch and once the craft is in orbit.

It is possible to become an environmental tester through joining a company as a general technician and working your way through to that position. In general, testers need to have a fair bit of knowledge about how the product is put together and what the performance criteria are for that product. This can really only be picked up through experience within individual companies.

 Highs: Designing new tests for specific products.

Lows: Can sometimes feel left out of the design and build process.

Rocket builder

The space race is still on. Not only are countries sending probes out into space in order to study our celestial neighbours, but the ever expanding communications industry means companies are very interested in buying satellites which can receive information from ground level and beam it around the world. These satellites need to orbit the earth at a distance of about 22,000 miles in a geo-stationary orbit which means they stay fixed over a specific point on the ground. While the industry is relatively small, there are many companies that contribute to spacecraft technology. The industry also enjoys a fair amount of crossover with work in the aeroplane industry – indeed, any area which uses high-end technology.

A client may present a company with certain specifications for a satellite such as period of use, position of orbit and accuracy for communicating with stations on the ground. It is up to the design and build team to create that satellite so it can be launched into space on top of a powerful rocket and function perfectly once it has achieved its orbit. The space engineers who do this are generally split between the two functions of structure and propulsion.

Carbon fibre panels are frequently used for the structure, being both light and strong. The satellite must be designed to endure extremes of temperature – sometimes being subject to the full force of the sun on one side and the extreme cold of deep space on the other. Special conductors are fitted to take the heat away from the satellite and ensure the temperature does not rise too high. Propulsion systems work by squirting hydrazine gas out of nozzles on board the craft. In all aspects of putting the satellite together, there is always a pay-off between features of the technology. One component may be strong but too heavy, another may be light enough but prone to overheating. The designers and engineers need to find the best solution.

Apprenticeships and training schemes are accessible to school-leavers so it is possible to start out as a machine operator and work to achieve a high level of competence and speciality in one area. You should always remember that while technical knowledge is important to the work, being able to operate as part of a team is crucial.

 Highs: Making new advances in space technology.

 Lows: There are only a few companies specializing specifically in space technology and finding promotion can be difficult.

Mission control manager

Once a satellite has been built, it is up to mission control to see that it achieves its intended geo-stationary orbit above the earth. To do this, flight dynamic technologists and other experts will control the satellite once it has blasted off from the launch pad and see that the craft moves into the right position. The flight dynamics team are responsible for the journey the satellite takes, but there will also be specialists on hand concerned with other functions of the satellite such as the deployment of antennae and solar panels.

Overseeing these teams is the mission control manager. This person is responsible for the success of the entire flight. He or she will give the go-ahead for actions to be taken by members of the control team and if problems occur, it is up to the manager to see each incident is dealt with without jeopardizing the flight. The manager's job is therefore a people-oriented one – taking a step back from the situation and facilitating the experts to apply their thinking to a problem.

This is not to say mission control managers do not have technical skills – on the contrary, they will have between ten and twenty years experience of working with satellites. It is this knowledge that enables them to manage the entire project. They may have started their career working in the flight dynamics area of the business – essentially number crunching work to determine when and where propulsion systems should be used to move the craft into orbit.

Their extensive experience in the business will make them aware of time factors relating to the project and they will know where to look for solutions. The launch mission period itself may last only two or three weeks, but the mission control team will have spent many years preparing for the launch, putting procedures into place to launch the craft and to cater for any problems that may emerge.

Highs: Commanding the team that gets the satellite into orbit.

 Lows: Some mission control related work is relatively mundane number crunching, but it is good to do since it gives you the knowledge of how satellites work.

Weather forecaster

There are two types of weather forecaster and consequently two broad paths to achieving the post. The first kind of forecaster is essentially a radio or TV presenter – someone who knows very little about forecasting and meteorology itself but is presentable, enthusiastic and able to read it out clearly. While many of the more established weather services will use qualified forecasters – see below – the rapidly increasing number of media channels could mean it becomes very easy to give weather reports for viewers or listeners on the radio without actually knowing anything about why it is raining in the first place.

Real qualified weather forecasters are employed in the UK by the Meteorological Office, usually referred to as the Met Office (tel: 01344 856287 or www.met-office.gov.uk). All the forecasters seen and heard on the BBC come directly from the Met Office; however, this is only the tip of the iceberg when it comes to forecasting jobs. The Met Office was established in 1854 to provide information on the wind and sea currents for mariners and to further the understanding of meteorology. Today, it provides services to the public and to governmental departments including the Department of the Environment, Transport and the Regions and even to the armed forces operating around the world.

Within the office, employees work under civil servant conditions as forecasters, weather observers, researchers and technical staff. There are also commercial marketing and sales staff whose job it is to push the office's services to new client areas. Forecasters need to have qualifications in meteorology, but can be employed with high-level science qualifications and receive specific training once they are employed.

The office supplies 3,000 tailored forecasts and briefings to customers every day covering different time periods and geographical areas. 'Nowcasts' cover the weather for the next

6 hours, short range from 6 hours to 3 days, medium range 3–10 days and the monthly prospect covers 10–15 days or 15–30 days. A seasonal forecast predicts conditions 3–6 months ahead while climate predictions offer information projected over the next 10 – 100 years. This latter forecast is particularly important to organizations such as the DETR and environmental groups who can use the information to help campaign to reduce global warming.

 Highs: Interpreting complex data to produce a forecast for specific clients.

 Lows: Irregular hours.

This is Entertainment

The entertainment world offers both the most diverse range of jobs of any sector and the most uncertain job market. Whether you want to act, direct films, help behind the scenes at pop gigs or work as a children's entertainer, success in the workplace will always be dependent on the current tastes of your audience.

Competition for jobs in the sector is fierce with many employees getting work because of who they know rather than what they know. Getting into the industry can mean a long period of knocking on doors and being knocked back. Even if a level of success is achieved, a sudden change in fashion or a bad piece of press can lead to disaster and unemployment.

In this section, entertaining people is taken beyond stage, screen and pop music. People today have more leisure time and are constantly searching for new and satisfying ways of filling in that time. The leisure industry is therefore an innovative area, welcoming new ideas which will attract large numbers of customers and audience.

The roadie/road crew

Road crew work in many areas of live performance, touring with everyone from children's theatre shows to rock groups to opera companies. A tour may be national or international covering many different continents. Some of the road crew positions – lighting technician, sound operator and so on – are highly qualified posts demanding a great deal of knowledge. At the other end of the scale, some roadies are employed simply to shift the heavy equipment off the transport trucks and into the venues. Whatever the position, the road crew must have the physical and mental stamina to cope with life on the road, working with the same people night after night and moving from venue to venue.

The easiest way to become a roadie is to be best mates with a group who are going on tour. Certainly new groups – theatre companies and music groups – get their friends to help them out and paid work can eventually come as a consequence of this. If you do not know any groups directly, you may be able to get into the business via the venues where they play. You will learn a lot from simply watching different groups coming into the venue and there will always be the need for an extra pair of hands. Failing that, the local music shop is also a good place to make contacts and may display advertisements to recruit helpful dogsbodies.

The work can be hard but is also a lot of fun. Touring artists often explain that they do not see much of the places where they are touring because they are spending so long on the road and setting up for the show. This is equally true for the road crew. At the same time, there is usually a great atmosphere backstage and plenty of parties to go to after the show.

Road crew often find themselves doing more than one job – particularly for theatre companies. While the music industry clearly marks who is responsible for which aspect of the show, a member of the theatrical road crew may be rigging lights one moment and sorting out costumes the next. In general, the smaller the touring operation is, the more work you will be expected to do and the more experienced you will need to be.

 Highs: Travel and working closely as a team.

Lows: The work can be exhausting and involves very long hours.

Sign/banner painter

Painting and drawing do not have to be something that you only enjoy in your spare time. With a bit of lateral thinking you can make a healthy living out of your art. Working artists do exist and they are not all waiting for a response from the Arts Council regarding the grant for which they have applied.

Sign and banner painters work for all sorts of customers. They may produce work for high street shops, for stalls at fairs and festivals or advertising banners for special events. Sometimes the work is fairly straightforward – for example, a mobile catering company is looking for a flag to advertise their location. But there can be more interesting and creative projects. Organizations may employ artists to create murals in and on their buildings, either as advertisements or simply to brighten the place up. A hospital might commission a mural, for example, to go inside a children's ward or along the corridors.

Finding these opportunities is not straightforward and it will be up to you to seek out employers rather than waiting for them to appear. You can suggest projects for yourself – show a local shop what kind of work you can do and give them a few examples of how you could change their own appearance. If the local hospital needs a coat of paint, make enquiries and find out if you can help. Whenever your work appears in a public place it will generate further interest in your work for the future.

Banner and sign painters need to be able to communicate well with their clients to discuss precisely what design they would like. At the same time the artist may have to work alongside the people who use those places – the patients and doctors in a hospital for instance. There may even be the chance to run workshops to discuss possible designs with the people who will see the painting every day. To this end, banner and sign painting is as much about working with others as it is about being technically proficient as an artist.

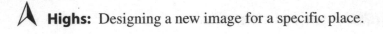

Highs: Designing a new image for a specific place.

Lows: Convincing the right people that it is a good idea can be hard work.

Museum performer/guide

Museums used to have a bad image. They were stuffy places predominantly full of 'old stuff' locked away under glass cabinets at which the general public could only gaze. However, many of today's museums provide a more interactive experience. These establishments have realized they are now in competition against other attractions in towns and cities – cinemas, theatres and gaming arcades. At the same time, exhibitions such as the Granada Studios Tour in Manchester have presented more contemporary subjects to the public, requiring a more innovative approach to creating an exhibition.

As a result, many venues employ performers to guide the public around the site, giving them specific information and entertaining them – usually all at the same time. There can be specific roles to take – the Granada Studios tour for example, includes a special stage show in which sound effects are demonstrated. Alternatively, your work may be more as a tour guide – explaining and demonstrating the use of certain exhibits. In both cases, the work requires a high level of performance skills to communicate the right information to your customers and ensure they do not get bored and wander off somewhere else.

Opening hours for museums mean the work can be done in fairly regular and predictable shifts, but since museums realize they are employing actors they are happy to allow time off for auditions or even extended periods of leave for rehearsals and performances. In some cases, contracts may be for a limited period of time, just so that the performers do not become bored or complacent about the work.

This kind of work can easily be extended into other tour guide activities. Every major town in the UK will have a tourist board or information centre and they usually require guides – whether for walking tours, tours of pubs, ghost tours or even on open-top buses. As long as you are able to retain a certain amount of knowledge on a subject and can communicate that knowledge in an entertaining way you will be able to guide groups of people around anything.

 Highs: Creating an entertaining approach to being a tour guide.

 Lows: Tours may be repetitive and dealing with the public can be very tiring.

Puppeteer

Puppetry means more than *Punch and Judy*. Today's puppet based performances are frequently the most innovative and affecting pieces of theatre around. Identified for the main part with children's theatre there are also many adult puppet theatres offering intriguing and imaginative pieces of work. There is an international audience for this work and regular puppetry festivals held all over the world. Puppets also play a part in street theatre or carnivals, with puppeteers building and operating huge marionettes which tower above their audiences. Puppeteers also work on the small and big screen – not simply with programmes such as *Sesame Street* and the *Muppets*, but in creating leading characters for many block-buster movies as monsters or aliens.

It is not necessary to have had a theatrical background to work with puppets. You may have an interest in textiles or craft activities. Whatever the case you will need a good imagination and sufficient practical skills to design and assemble your own creations. Puppets can be made using a wide range of materials – from wood and cloth through to rubber latex or simply paper silhouettes. As with all performance-related work, the most likely way into this area of work is through voluntary work and proving your worth through making your own creations. Puppeteers must be able to work with other people, understanding the design and concept of the performance or show that the puppets will be used for. They must be able to work to deadlines creating their puppets and have a good level of physical coordination to be able to operate the puppets successfully.

Puppets have also been used for educational purposes – one puppeteer found herself working for the local leisure centre creating floating puppets which would teach children about safety in water. Puppets have also been used therapeutically when working with children who have suffered trauma. The children found it easier to talk about their experiences using the puppets rather than relating their experiences directly.

 Highs: Creating new characters and shows.

 Lows: Work can be erratic, pay is not always good and puppeteers may find themselves taking on less inspiring projects in order to pay the rent.

Circus performer

The circus used to be a family business. The skills, show-manship and even the big top would stay in the family, handed down from generation to generation. This is now no longer the case. Firstly, the circus has moved away from being a trained animal spectacle to being a people-oriented show of skills. From the Chinese and Russian State Circuses, to Circus Oz and the work of Archaos and the Circus of Horrors, this form of entertainment has been redefined, bringing in new talent and creating new shows.

The idea behind Archaos and the Circus of Horrors was to use the traditional circus structure   the big top and the show-manship   but to inject it with a contemporary anarchic element – punk rock and horror show styles. There would still be clowns and jugglers, but now they would chase one another with chain-saws and juggle fish while riding motorbikes. Sure there would be a trapeze act, but the trapeze would be suspended from an industrial crane. In short, animals were taken out of the equation and imagination was brought in.

Circus skills are used in many other areas of the entertainment industry. They are great for street entertainment and unicyclists and jugglers are always to be found at Covent Garden in London or whenever there is a suitable festival in the UK. Performers can also find work on TV and the stage when performances require their special skills.

Getting these skills has become relatively easy. There are no end of workshops teaching you how to juggle or do the diablo. There are even sessions which will teach high wire and trapeze acts or clowning techniques. There is now even a Circus College in London which offers a BTEC course in circus skills. Once you have learned the basics, you can then experiment with your skills and extend your performance repertoire. You will find imagination and originality are treasured in this field. And once you have established yourself as a competent performer you will be able to make money through running your own classes and passing the skills on to the next generation.

 Highs: Entertaining people with something they cannot do.

Lows: Work can be erratic and audiences can vary.

Montage/demontage crew

A classic summer job, montage staff are employed to travel around foreign campsites putting up tents (montage) at the beginning of the summer season and taking them down (demontage) at the end of the season. A doddle. And even better than that, a doddle you can almost treat as a fully paid holiday.

The reason this job exists is that some holidaymakers like the idea of camping in Europe, but either do not have their own tent or cannot face the idea of putting it up themselves. Instead, a holiday company will book a ready-erected tent for them and kit it out with as many mod cons as possible – a fridge, a cooker, beds, etc. All the holidaymakers need to do is drive to their holiday site and take up residency in their very own ready-made tent. Before the season begins, therefore, the holiday companies must find a bunch of people who will go and put up the tents, plug in all the necessary appliances and ensure the sites are ready for the holidaymakers.

It can be hard and tiring work. The tents will have been in storage over the winter together with all the other equipment, resulting in bent poles, damaged canvases and mouldy fridges. Pitching the tents is only part of the process. All the equipment must be cleaned, sorted and replaced if there is anything missing. However, it can be a very enjoyable way to spend a few weeks or months – as long as the weather is good and you find yourself working with a nice bunch of fellow montage workers.

If you are lucky and want to stay for the entire season you may be able to get work as a site host or a crèche attendant. This way, once you have put all the tents up you will be left on a campsite ready for the first holiday arrivals. Site hosts are not simply there to ensure the holidaymakers have a good time, but since the sites are loaned from the owner of the campsite they may need to liaise with them as well. In such cases it can be useful to have foreign language skills.

▲ **Highs:** Working abroad and travelling.

▼ **Lows:** Can be hard manual labour.

Karaoke party host

Coming live to a venue near you, the karaoke party is a chance for everyone to get up and strut their stuff, taking their dreams of pop stardom one stage further than standing in front of their bedroom mirror with a hairbrush. The basic format is this: karaoke host turns up at party venue – or even just a room in a pub – bringing a public address (PA) system, a TV screen or two and an extensive catalogue of laser discs which contain the music and the words to countless popular songs.

People at the party or in the pub select a song they would like to have a go at, take the microphone and sing along to the tune following the words displayed on the TV screen. As a result, everyone falls about laughing because they are so awful or they spend the rest of the night being very quiet and occasionally saying 'They should be a professional singer, you know?'

If you do not have the picture yet, being a karaoke host requires an enormous amount of self-confidence (some might say lack of self-consciousness) as it is up to you to raise the party spirit, inspire the crowd and encourage them to get up on stage and perform. This task can vary from being like trying to get blood from a stone to being a matter of crowd control – depending on how forthcoming the audience is. You will have to do the first song yourself to show how it is done – or possibly the first hour if the audience prove reluctant – or even the entire night if it does not go very well. You do not need to have professional training but as the host you should not really go anywhere near the equipment without an average singing voice and an extrovert personality.

A bit of market research – around pubs, clubs and private parties – will put you in the picture as to how many shows you could expect to do every month and you may find enough regular engagements to justify the large investment in your own equipment. Alternatively, there are entertainment agencies who offer such shows and you may do better tracking one of these down and seeking employment with them. In London, there is now a club specifically devoted to karaoke. Private rooms equipped with their own machines can be booked by groups of people, allowing them to sing badly at each other without distressing other members of the public.

Highs: Meeting people and putting on a show.

Lows: Having to endure another dreadful version of Robbie Williams' 'Angels'.

TV/film extra

Also known as 'background artists' these are the people you see hanging around the pub on TV when the leading actor is arguing with the barman. They just happen to be passing when the hero of the film is running down the street – glimpsed for a moment and then gone forever. In spite of this brevity, being an extra is still a skilled job and workers will have had some level of training as well as being members of the actors' union Equity. It is not very easy to act naturally and background artists may need to repeat precise actions over and over again for the needs of shooting. Getting yourself into the frame is usually a matter of word of mouth and keeping your eyes peeled for useful advertisements. Papers like *The Stage* carry notifications of auditions but approach with extreme caution any agencies that offer to register you for extras work for a fee. In recent years, many of these operations have simply proved to be scams with the so-called agency taking fees from people and not doing anything to get them work.

Being an extra can be far removed from the bright lights of Hollywood. Extras may find themselves hanging around for long periods of time doing nothing while the film crew set up a shot and try to get the material they want. There is the chance that you will be selected for a particular role as an extra – you may have to interact with the lead characters or you may be a definite character who stands out from the crowd. If you are identifiable in one shot you may find you are released from the rest of the day's shooting – the next shot could be ruined if you appear to be in two places at once.

It is imperative that you are well behaved on set and do exactly what you are told. It is not simply a question of getting the camera shot right; there is often very heavy equipment or scaffolding in use on a film set that can be dangerous. Budding actors should beware of doing too much extra work. It should not be viewed as a path to landing major roles and inevitably could be limiting for your career if producers and casting directors perceive you only as background cast.

 Highs: Appearing on screen and being part of the making of a film.

Lows: A lot of waiting around for a very short appearance in a production.

Club promoter/DJ

What to do on a Saturday night is now a complex question. The proliferation of new club nights and dance music genres has blown this area of the nightlife industry wide open. Moreover, in the UK's larger cities it has become a seven-days-a-week business with clubs opening every night playing the music the clubbers want to hear. The fact is, anyone can set up his or her own club night on some scale or other. If the music is right and the crowds enjoy the evening, there is no limit to how far the club night can go – successful promoters and DJs even produce their own merchandise to go with the club – clothing and compilation records of music.

However, creating your own club and ensuring it is full of enthusiastic revellers is a time-consuming and exhausting affair. First you have to find a venue. You may be able to talk a club or café into giving you an evening (usually a quiet evening) on which to try your hand, but it could mean hiring the upstairs function room in a local pub. You need to have a clear idea of what the night is going to consist of – what kind of people you want to attract, what music will be played and so on. All this will affect the way you put the night together, the image of the club and the promotional work you need to do to get people there.

Alongside the hard work, however, putting a club night together can be extremely good fun and enables you to work with lots of different people on one project. There may be visual artists you can use to provide wall hangings, video and film artists who can create projections to accompany the music and lighting designers who will help to generate the right atmosphere in the venue. You may have a good enough record collection and enough experience to DJ yourself, but you should have guest DJs from time to time who will provide different music and could even be an additional draw for the crowd. This could mean finding the finance to pay those DJs – finance which inevitably comes from the people who walk through the door.

You are going to need a fair amount of money up front to set up your club. Venue hire, sound and light hire and even the DJs will want paying before you have started to count up the cash at the front door. Ensuring you do not lose money on the event means you need to set door prices that will cover your expenses when you get a certain number of clubbers in. Get more numbers than that and you start making money. If you are successful in one venue you can offer the night to other places and begin to negotiate better terms for yourself. As you play in bigger venues the door takings will rise while your operating costs stay basically the same.

 Highs: You create a place that you enjoy and others do too.

 Lows: Arranging everything – it is best to do this in a team and make sure everyone pulls their weight.

TV researcher

If you want to get into TV, here is the first rung on the ladder. Researchers are involved in all kinds of programmes – documentaries, quiz shows and even dramas. Put simply, researchers spend their time finding facts, people, places, subjects – everything and anything that is needed for the TV programme they are working on.

The actual workplace will depend on the show for which you are working. In some cases, researching is a phone-based occupation, requiring you to work from a production office spending all day on the phone trying to track down certain people. Alternatively you may be working on a travel programme or history show, in which case the job is likely to take you farther afield. However it is done, researchers take the information they have tracked down and report back to the programme's producer or director so they can decide how best to use the material in the show. For some programmes, researchers may even brief the show's presenter, perhaps in an interview situation so the presenter knows what questions they should ask an interviewee.

In drama, researchers are used to provide detailed backgrounds to storylines. Contemporary crime stories may require details about police procedure or forensic information; there may be historical information required to help the costume and design department working on a period drama. Researchers may even help actors and actresses understand their roles.

To be a good researcher you need to be enthusiastic and outgoing. You should not be afraid to ask questions – even if they appear to be stupid or if they are difficult to ask. You must be able to work on your own initiative as well as understanding precisely what your producer or director wants. You will also need to be patient and tactful – sources may be nervous about where their information will end up while at the same time the TV industry is full of clashing egos.

As a researcher, you will see how the TV industry fits together and how programmes are made. With this information and experience, you will be able to graduate to higher ranks within the profession in production or post-production roles. Rates of pay may initially be low or even non-existent but researching gives you plenty of room to manoeuvre as you climb up the ladder.

 Highs: Seeing your work on TV.

Lows: Work can be very high pressure with long hours, short deadlines and exacting producers.

Location manager

This job is one of the more high-pressured roles within TV but can be rewarding both financially and personally. Location managers are attached to specific TV programmes to find suitable locations in which they can be recorded. A single episode of a drama, for example, could mean a list of requirements covering several different interior and exterior locations. The location manager must go out and find places which match these requirements, making sure the owners or residents are willing to let their lives be disrupted by a few days of filming.

Once these places have been found, the location manager's job is still not done. When filming takes place the manager is responsible for every aspect of the location – from ensuring the production vehicles have space to park to cleaning up the mess left by the film crew at the end of the day. Location managers need to anticipate problems which may arise during the shoot and ensure filming runs smoothly. They may need to inform the local police that filming is taking place, ask the locals to keep the noise down during recording or deal with the spectators who are naturally drawn by the appearance of a film crew.

Dealing with all these elements can make location management a nightmare of a job, but it also has its rewards. The manager gets to meet lots of interesting people both in and outside the TV industry and they can make a clear and strong contribution to the look and feel of a show. The manager is involved at the heart of producing the finished show.

No one would get a job in location management as soon as he or she enters the TV profession – it is a role that requires an appreciation of the whole production process. Some may become location managers after working their way through the production ranks – beginning as a runner, for example, who literally runs around the film unit carrying out different jobs as required. Perhaps the quickest route to this work is through the

Skillset training course (tel: 020 7534 5300) where students receive a grounding in all areas of TV production in a shorter period of time.

 Highs: A vital role in TV and film, the location spotter has massive responsibilities.

Lows: Long hours and very stressful work.

Performance artist

The term performance artist is usually applied to performers whose work does not seem to fit in any other category – theatre, dance or visual arts. They will sometimes perform in a conventional theatre space but could essentially stage an event wherever they feel inclined – be it an art gallery, a public space or a car park. Similarly they may not restrict themselves to one single mode of expression. A single show could comprise music, song, dance and visual art. But how is it possible to make money through this kind of performance?

To begin with, there are a number of festivals, nationally and internationally, where new work is commissioned from artists. These may be dedicated art festivals or more general festivities based around a geographic location or a calendar event. Artists may find they are able to suggest, create and perform unique shows which bring something special to the event. One group of performance artists, for example, specialize in a show in which they dress in silver tubes, moving and intersecting with one another to the delight of audiences. They are a particular hit with public and street festivals. Another troop known as 'The Cone Heads' (who do have pointy heads) interact and improvise with festival crowds, causing curiosity and laughter.

Artists can find work in unlikely places. Private companies sometimes employ artists and writers to work with their customers and employees to bring something different to their everyday business. Poets and writers in residence, for example, offer activities which put a different spin on working the day-to-day grind, while on-site entertainment can help raise morale.

Finding out where these opportunities exist is a question of getting yourself involved in the artistic world. There are a number of useful news groups and mailing lists on the Internet where performers share information about upcoming bursaries and festivals. Alternatively, getting yourself involved in a performance group will provide you with first-hand knowledge of where to look for funding. Being a successful artist is never going to mean lots of money but by applying your talent to many different circumstances – from festivals to workplaces – it is possible to do what you want to do without starving.

 Highs: Turning in a good performance and finding new performance areas.

 Lows: Poverty.

Fairground operator

Travelling funfair rides are generally a family business, run by people who are born and brought up in the nomadic life. It is a gruelling life with few rewards – living out of caravans, setting up and taking down rides in all weathers and making just enough money to get by. But for those who enjoy the fun of the fair and love people to scream if they want to go faster, there is an alternative. The rise of the theme park has made it possible to find full- and part-time jobs in running amusement rides.

Many theme parks are owned by national companies who have resorts and attractions across the country and internationally. Each year these parks are in competition with one another, trying to attract more customers through more incredible rides or by offering more exciting experiences. These experiences may include elements such as themed hotels – as seen at Alton Towers – or all-in-one travel packages such as those offered by Disney. Alongside the rides at a place like Disney, entertainers and character performers are employed to entertain visitors as they move from ride to ride.

In whatever context they work, ride operators are employed to make sure the riders are safely fastened in their seats before the ride begins. They must ensure the attraction is safe before each ride and know what to do if there are any problems. They may also need to advise customers not to take the ride should height or health restrictions apply.

There may be smaller, more locally based resorts where you can work alongside fairground attractions. The scale of operation here means you are likely to have more responsibility for the site than you would being employed by a large company and so understandably you will need a wider variety of skills to do the job.

The rides themselves are designed and constructed by specialist construction firms. Artists and designers working here require specialist engineering skills to ensure the ride works safely and consistently. Designers can also find work in creating the theme park environment in which these rides will be positioned. Designed properly it should be possible for onlookers to feel involved with the ride even if they do not get on board.

 Highs: Giving customers a unique experience.

Lows: Working in all weathers and sometimes the work can be repetitive.

Stand-up comedian

A few years ago comedy was billed as the new rock and roll. Anyone could get on stage and do their 10 minutes and if they were good, fame and fortune were waiting. All you needed were enough guts to get up there and do it in the first place. Today the opportunity for getting up and showing off still exists, but the comedy scene is now awash with 'wannabe' comedians so becoming a top stand-up comic requires limitless enthusiasm, bags of commitment and not a little talent.

London has a thriving comedy circuit of small pub rooms and a few dedicated clubs where new comedians can get up and try to make people laugh. Some of these places have a proper PA system and microphone; other places have nothing more than a single amplifier and speaker while others will not even bother with lights or microphones at all. The aspiring comedian travels round all these venues many times, doing as many gigs as possible and trying to impress the audience and the bookers – the club owners – alike. In general, these spots last for 5–10 minutes but even this can seem like an eternity to the comic who has bad material.

The comic must show bookers that they are keen to improve their act, that they are trying new things out and that they want to succeed in the business. Gradually, they may be offered other 'open mic' slots on more high profile dates. They may eventually start getting paid gigs from bookers who like their act. Many stand-ups go to the Edinburgh Festival each year, usually financing their own shows to promote their talent. Edinburgh can be seen as a trade fair for bookers and there may be many people there on the lookout for new talent to develop TV or radio shows.

To be successful in the world of stand-up you need a certain amount of chance and luck as well as talent and skill. You need to be in the right place at the right time and talking to the right people. It can appear that comedians – again like pop stars – are overnight successes, but frequently such overnight success has been preceded by many years of toil doing hard gigs, dying on stage and wondering whether what you are doing is actually funny at all.

 Highs: Having a good night on stage where everyone loves you.

 Lows: Having to phone round venues again in order to book more gigs.

Stunt person

As everyone knows, movie stars hardly ever do their own stunts. It may appear that Pierce Brosnan is able to drive incredibly fast cars without crashing, leap from buildings without hurting himself and so on, but as soon as the difficult bit comes along, the actor is led to the safety of his Winnebago trailer while the stunt person is brought on to do the dangerous stuff.

It is a very skilled profession. Stunt people are generally fit and may be skilled in martial arts – judo and so on – in order to be able to fight safely and to fall over convincingly without hurting themselves. For more complex stunts, involving vehicles for example, the qualified stunt person will design the stunt and ensure all the equipment is ready and in good condition before any action takes place. They are responsible for the safety of the stunt since it is usually they who get hurt if anything goes wrong.

Newcomers to the industry must gain an amount of experience working alongside qualified stunt people. You can find contact details of stunt people in various media directories – the *White Book* being the most informative. All stunt performers must be listed on the Register of Stunt Performers and Arrangers. Probationary membership lasts three years during which time the probationer works alongside a fully registered member until their work is assessed and their application for full membership considered. Having become a full member, stunt performers must then work for another two years in the industry before becoming a stunt arranger, which means they can design stunts for other actors and performers. In this way, while some level of technique can be gained through formal training in martial arts and so on, the profession is generally handed on through generations of stunt performers with newcomers learning old tricks from their predecessors.

Stunt work is becoming more specialist. There are stunt performers who are particularly skilled at arranging airborne stunts, while others will be more experienced in driving work. Just as the film industry is an international business, stunt performers can find themselves working all over the world.

Highs: Creating and filming a new or innovative stunt.

Lows: Low job security – both out of work and in work!

Role-player/mystery shopper

Used for the training and assessment of staff, role players and mystery shoppers have one of the more devious jobs in the world of business and retail. Training staff to deal with customers or indeed, training staff to deal with other members of staff, is important to companies which want to put the customer first and maximize the efficiency of their organization. Role players are employed either covertly or explicitly to help employers assess the way their employees handle customers and fellow members of staff. If used explicitly the employee realizes the interview is a test and will try to behave appropriately, showing off their people skills to the full. Such an interview could be used as part of a recruitment test or may simply be there to assess the employee's skills and suggest areas for improvement. In some cases the interview may be stopped and restarted for the employee to try different approaches to the same problem.

Alternatively, the employee may have no idea that the person they are dealing with is not a 'real' member of the public. A mystery shopper may be used to carry out a specific transaction with a member of staff and to report back on how effectively they dealt with the situation. Mystery shoppers could be used by the employing organization or may be sent by a third party in order to survey the quality of services on offer from a variety of suppliers. A magazine could review the customer service standards of a number of chemists, for example, measuring them for knowledge and helpfulness.

Role-playing is particularly common in the financial world where there are many rules and regulations that must be observed by suppliers when dealing with customers. There are definite pieces of information which have to be stated to and understood by the customer when dealing with mortgages, for example. Often, the outcome of a role-play interview will affect the future career of an individual so it is important that the role-player should be impartial and fair when conducting an interview – not just creating problems for the sake of it.

There are a few role-playing agencies in the UK who look to take on actors as role-players. However, you may also be able to find work by approaching companies directly. The training department of retail banks may indicate whether they use role-players for developing their staff.

 Highs: Able to use acting skills in a constructive way.

Lows: Acting out the same role can become boring.

Professional look-alike

You will need an amount of good luck in the looks department to be successful at this job. At the same time simply looking like someone famous is not guaranteed to earn you a living. You will need to be able to enter into the spirit of the person you look like – creating an entire performance that makes your act believable and helps people enjoy what you do. You will need to act and perform. You may need to sing or even make public speeches.

Look-alikes are used on a wide range of occasions. They may be used for corporate events, advertising campaigns, modelling work or for public engagements. They might appear to liven up private parties and increasingly there is a trend for look-alike and sound-alike 'tribute' bands playing the music of many popular groups. A quick scan of the back page of *The Stage* newspaper reveals the number of look-alikes available – royalty, TV personalities, film stars, both alive and dead – as well as tribute bands to *The Beatles*, *ABBA* and many others. Alarmingly, sound-alike bands are sprouting up playing the songs of contemporary artists – there is already a *Steps* tribute band to join *U2* tribute bands and others. *The Stage* is also a good source to find the contact details of agencies and management companies who deal with look-alikes.

Being a look-alike can mean international work and film work. You may find yourself working long hours just as any performer and you may find the constant act of being someone else very tiring. Some look-alikes find it frustrating that they cannot actually get any work as themselves – they must always appear as their look-alike. Success here is absolutely linked to the popularity of the character you are playing. If they fall out of favour or are forgotten then you are likely to be out of work. Moreover, it can be difficult – although not impossible – to switch to being a different, more popular look-alike. When their star finally falls, some look-alikes remain in the entertainment business, becoming agents and artist managers themselves.

Highs: Being treated as a famous person.

Lows: Not being wanted to perform as you; typecasting.

Here's Health

I nterest in complementary medicine has been increasing over many years as individuals search out new approaches and treatments that fit their lifestyle. While the British Medical Association (BMA) may not recognize some of these treatments, they are gaining popularity among general practitioners, some of whom have even trained in these subjects and are able to offer them alongside the usual service. In the absence of recognition from the BMA and exclusion from National Health Service (NHS) delivery, many areas of complementary medicine now have their own regulatory bodies, recognizing training centres that specialize in that area of medicine and individuals qualified to practise. These organizations should be your first port of call for finding out more about the area of treatment in which you are interested and how you can get started.

You should be aware of a few points surrounding this area of work. Firstly, there is usually a great deal of training involved requiring large amounts of your time, energy and finance. Secondly, these practices still require a high standard of academic work especially in the area of human biology. It is impossible to work in any complementary medical practice without understanding how the body works. Thirdly, many – but not all – of the people who do take up a job as a practitioner in alternative medicine do so as a second career. This is partly due to the financial requirement and partly because of the experience and life skills one needs in order to be a successful practitioner in this area. Practitioners need a level of maturity – partly in order to gain the confidence of their patients – which school-leavers may find hard to demonstrate.

Finally, being a successful practitioner requires another completely different set of skills. Alternative and complementary medical practitioners tend to be self-employed, running individual practices from home if not from dedicated surgeries. The individual must therefore be able to be their own boss, managing the financial and promotional side of the activity and ensuring the work does not take over their entire lives. A number of practitioners set up surgeries with each other in order to spread the task of attracting patients, splitting overheads and running costs.

Chiropodist

Many people pay no attention to their feet. They just assume the bits on the end of their legs will take care of themselves. However, healthy feet are often the key to an individual's all-round happiness. If walking is uncomfortable then the whole posture of an individual can be affected. Chiropodists have been around for many years taking care of all medical problems associated with the feet. They will remove bunions, treat calluses and verrucas or simply give the foot a clean-up and massage. Their work can prevent ingrowing toenails and help people walk properly and in comfort.

Chiropodists can work from dedicated private clinics or may operate a mobile service, travelling to patients with their own equipment and carrying out their work in the patient's home. Unsurprisingly patients tend to be old people – pensioners who are no longer able to look after their feet and who may suffer from problems due to walking badly. However, chiropody has gained some popularity with younger people, keen to get the benefits of well looked after feet. Chiropodists may also work in the sports world and even the theatre – professional ballet dancers for example, rely on their feet for their livelihood and need help and support to look after them.

A full medical qualification is not necessary for the work, but it is necessary to have scientific knowledge at the GCSE level before you will be accepted on a training course. Many colleges run chiropody programmes – both residential and distance learning – and the Scholl organization also runs training programmes based around their network of high street shops. Training is split between the classroom and on-the-job practice – watching how it is done and then practising under the watchful eye of a professional.

Chiropodists must be very good communicators, able to reassure and talk to their patients while carrying out the work.

Chiropodists should also be aware that the condition of the feet could be symptomatic of a greater problem – from the wrong type of footwear to more serious medical conditions.

 Highs: Watching someone who has hobbled into the chiropodist's chair walk comfortably away.

Lows: Extracting eight bunions in one go.

Trichologist

Trichology is the diagnosis and treatment of diseases and disorders of the hair and scalp. This does not just mean trying to come up with the best cure for baldness. In the trichologist's work, the health of the skin is as important as the hair and they may need to deal with flaky or oily skin conditions as well as hair loss. Few people realize the importance of their hair – it may be primarily a cosmetic feature, but as such, it plays an important part in personal presentation. As a result, problems in this area can be acutely embarrassing, leading to low self-esteem and even depression.

Trichologists work alone, or may set up clinics with other trichologists, but as they are self-employed they are responsible for advertising and attracting their own customers. Since hair plays such an important part in personal identity and presentation it is clear that practising trichologists must be extremely good with people in discussing problems and selecting the right treatment for them. Job satisfaction comes from treating the condition and seeing the improvement in the whole person, not just their hair.

The Institute of Trichologists (tel: 08706 070602) recognizes qualified individuals in this area and even runs its own three-year training course for new entrants. The course requires two A levels and at least a GCSE in one science-based subject. However, the Institute of Trichologists has recently introduced a foundation course which will take students without those qualifications to the standard required for the full course. The course itself covers biology, microscopy, organic and inorganic chemistry as well as special modules on the structure and make-up of the hair. It is distance learning for the first year with direct experience at a trichology clinic over the following two years. The profession attracts some young people and a few from hairdressing – it seems concern for the cosmetic side of the hair can lead to wanting to be able to treat the health of the hair too.

Highs: Helping to treat hair conditions and improving the appearance of people.

Lows: Some conditions are not treatable.

Herbalist

The knowledge and use of herbal remedies goes back over a century. As with many complementary medicines, herbalism takes a holistic approach to health and disease, addressing the entire body rather than simply identifying and treating symptoms alone. To this end, the herbalist begins treatment with a full consultation for each patient, gathering information about all aspects of their life. This information includes the individual's diet, habits and lifestyle as well as details of the specific complaint which led the patient to consult the herbalist in the first place.

Herbalism seeks to restore health in human beings through the use of medicinal plants. It is clearly a more 'natural' way of treating conditions than conventional courses of drugs and indeed herbalism avoids problems which can arise through adverse reactions to conventional treatment.

Training to become a herbalist is extensive and there are a number of colleges and universities that offer courses in this area. The College of Phytotherapy in East Sussex (Bucksteep Manor, Bodle Street Green, Near Hailsham, East Sussex, BN27 4RJ, tel: 01323 834800) runs a four-year full-time course towards a BSc in Phytotherapy – the entrance requirement for which is good GCSE passes including English and A level passes in at least two subjects. A part-time course has also been designed but this takes five years to complete. The course includes in-depth study of medicinal plants and their effects on the human body as well as their preparation and prescription. The herbalist also receives full training in consulting techniques and diagnosis to ensure they get the right information from patients to prescribe suitable treatment.

With such a long and therefore expensive training period, anyone who wants to enter this area of work must be passionate about herbalism, regarding it as a vocation rather than just a job.

Once qualified, herbalists may work as peripatetic doctors – travelling between patients and treating them on site – or they may establish their own surgery.

 Highs: Treating illness with nature.

 Lows: Herbalism is one of the less well-known areas of complementary medicine and you may experience a low number of patients.

Acupuncturist

While the practice of acupuncture still goes unregulated in the UK, it is good to know that regulatory bodies do exist. Between them, the British Acupuncture Council and the British Acupuncture Accreditation Board define and recognize standards for both education in and the practice of acupuncture. This is just as well since acupuncture is one of the more invasive treatments one can receive, consisting of the placing of needles in strategic areas of the body.

Acupuncture is based on traditional Chinese philosophy that health is based on the smooth and balanced flow of the body's motivating energy known as Qi. Qi flows through a series of meridians or channels beneath the skin and is made up of equal and opposite qualities – Yin and Yang. When Yin and Yang are unbalanced there may be illness within the patient. By inserting needles into the patient's body, the acupuncturist can stimulate the body's own healing responses and thus restore the natural balance. The flow of Qi could be disrupted by a number of different factors including emotional states such as anxiety, stress and grief or through more physical factors – poor nutrition, infections and trauma. Thus acupuncture can treat all manner of conditions within patients – helping to relieve pain, depression and even helping people overcome addictions to smoking, alcohol and food.

As in other areas of complementary medicine, acupuncture takes a holistic approach, treating the entire body rather than specific symptoms. The acupuncturist will therefore establish a clear case history before commencing treatment which could range from studying the shape and appearance of the tongue through to dietary and medical issues.

Many patients have preconceptions about what acupuncture involves and they may be nervous about what will happen. The acupuncturist will need to provide reassurance before commencing treatment. There are around 500 acupuncture points on the body, 100 of which are most commonly used and while needles are usually associated with the treatment, acupuncture can be used for babies and children simply through applying pressure to the relevant points.

There are many training centres that run a variety of courses in acupuncture up and down the country. The British Acupuncture Accreditation Board holds a list of recognized training centres and can be contacted on 020 8735 0466.

 Highs: Treating people in a different and interesting way.

Lows: Overcoming prejudice against this kind of treatment.

Hypnotherapist

Hypnosis is a trance state in which something unusual happens. Essentially, hypnotherapists make suggestions to an individual's mind in order to bring about a change in that person's behaviour. You have probably seen hypnotists on stage or TV putting members of their audience into a trance and then suggesting they are other people or that they should carry out certain activities. In hypnotherapy, the patient is placed into a similar suggestive state, but this is then used to address emotional, mental or even physical problems.

Some people feel hypnosis has something mysterious to it, but hypnotherapy is really about using the body's natural mechanisms for change and focusing them in order to benefit the individual. It is not possible to hypnotize someone against their will and once placed in that state the hypnotherapist must only address the issues required by the patient. In the case of smokers who wish to give up, they may place a suggestion in the patient's head that cigarettes taste particularly bad. They may give them another suggestion so that they automatically refuse cigarettes when they are offered. In both cases, the hypnotherapist is merely offering a technique to help support the patient's own will to give up smoking.

In the case of emotional problems, hypnotherapy can enable the patient to remember significant events from their past which could still be affecting their behaviour today. Under hypnosis this event can be replayed and suggestions made to counter the emotional response from that event.

Applying hypnosis is a skill that people can learn – indeed many doctors and dentists use hypnotherapy for the treatment of pain or anxiety during other treatments. Dealing with emotions and feelings at this level does require very particular people skills. Hypnotherapists must be good communicators and extremely patient with their clients. They must always be in control of the sessions they run and exude confidence to their patients.

 Highs: Enabling people to overcome problems.

Lows: You may suffer from the suspicion some people attach to hypnosis.

Osteopath

Osteopathy is a method of treatment based on the manipulation of the bones. The principles of osteopathy were founded by A T Still in the late 1800s. Still believed that many diseases and conditions of the body could be aided through the manipulation of the bones and muscles as this would directly affect the blood flow around the body. Indeed, research continues today to assess the direct benefits produced by osteopathic treatments.

Treatment from an osteopath begins with a thorough analysis of the patient's condition. This will comprise a physical examination as well as assessing the patient's dietary and living habits. Very often a patient's body language can tell the osteopath more about the patient's condition than the individual is able to report themselves.

Training to be an osteopath is a rigorous process, covering consultation and diagnosis backed up with a full knowledge of biology. Anatomy is studied in great detail as well as general pathology – that is, the way the body works – and nutrition. Treatment itself is referred to as the neuro-muscular technique and, clearly, students must have a sound grasp of how the body works before they start the hands-on work of manipulation. For this reason, potential osteopaths can look forward to at least three years of training before setting up in practice. They should ideally have three A level passes including Chemistry and Biology, although some colleges will allow entrants who can demonstrate similar levels of competency or experience without official qualifications.

Since treatment is a physical activity osteopaths must be very confident in themselves and with other people's bodies. You cannot feel nervous about treating patients and must be able to put them at their ease before, during and after treatment.

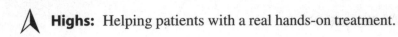

Highs: Helping patients with a real hands-on treatment.

Lows: Setting up your own practice and getting your own patients can be difficult and time consuming.

Homeopath

While the principles and practice of homeopathy date back some two hundred years, it is only in the last twenty years or so that formal structures have been introduced to this area of complementary medicine. Essentially, homeopathy entails treating disease by using small amounts of a medicine which in healthy persons would produce symptoms similar to that of the disease being treated. The popularity of this form of medicine – amongst patients and practitioners – has increased immensely over recent years, a fact which may in part be due to increased computer use. Database technology makes cross-referencing substances with the effects they have much easier, facilitating the homeopath's work. At the same time, electronic communication has brought together what was a diverse and widespread community of practitioners, allowing them to share and develop practice.

Like other complementary medical practitioners, the homeopath begins treatment by gathering information from the patient from all aspects of their life. While patients will attend with specific problems, the homeopath must take other symptoms and the patient's general condition into account. It is part of the homeopath's skill and art as to how this evidence is used. Trying to address too many symptoms may dilute the medicine's effect with the result that little progress is made in any one area. Having considered the patient's evidence, the homeopath will then select the medicine they consider will have the best result for that condition. Follow-up sessions may be set on a monthly basis for the homeopath to track the effect of the treatment with the patient and make further recommendations and prescriptions if required.

On a daily basis, the homeopath may hear the problems and conditions of lots of different patients. The homeopath must develop a way of empathizing with people – understanding their problems – while not getting too involved and being able to preserve their own personal space. They must maintain a professional distance and ensure that they are still paid and still attracting new patients to replace those who are satisfied with their treatment and ready for discharge.

There are over a dozen colleges around the country where homeopathy can be studied. The Society of Homeopaths (2 Atizan Road, Northampton NN1 4HU, tel: 01604 621400) is one of a few organizations that give professional recognition to homeopaths and they are involved with developing standards for education that will help prospective students to be certain of the standard of training they receive.

 Highs: Treating patient's conditions and enhancing their health.

Lows: It takes at least two years to establish a good homeopathic practice and around 80 per cent of trainees do not manage to create such ventures.

Bath ballistics maker

The cosmetics world has recently become a battlefield, with companies trying to outdo one another through the freshness and novelty value of cleansing products for the body, face, hair and hands. Out of this has come the bath ballistic – a ball made of bicarbonate and full of numerous natural, smelly, relaxing and skin nourishing ingredients. The ballistic is dropped into a running bath whereupon the bicarbonate fizzes and the ball disintegrates, spreading its oils, perfumes and nutrients through the water.

Creating ballistics in large numbers requires an efficient production line of enthusiastic workers. Each worker is supplied with the ingredients required for the ballistic they are making and it is their job to mix these together to the right consistency, put them into a mould and wait for them to set. Workers must be able to use their own initiative, ensuring the ballistics they make reach the usual standard for the product and changing the ingredients if they do not measure up. At the same time, it is unlikely that you will end up simply making ballistics all day. Cosmetics manufacturers produce a wide range of products so you will need to be a flexible worker, able to work on all the different lines and in different parts of the production process.

The ballistics themselves are designed and created by qualified trichologists and chemists, but there may be opportunities for training and development in this area for workers who show an interest. You should start by contacting the manufacturers direct – there may be vacancies within production or in the distribution and marketing side of the company. In many cases, companies are looking for original, off-the-wall approaches to marketing which will get the public revelling in their luxury bath products. Working as a ballistics maker on the production line will not immediately enable you to design your own bath products, but you will have the chance to rise through the ranks.

 Highs: Groovy product – and very nice-smelling work-place.

Lows: While you may be moved around the production process, you may still find the work repetitive.

Pest controller

It has been suggested that if a large bomb were dropped on the major cities of the world the only survivors would be the cockroaches. These insects can – and do – get everywhere and once an infestation begins they are extremely difficult to eradicate. However, they can spread dirt and germs and so represent a serious health risk if left to their own devices.

Pest controllers work in both commercial buildings – shops and offices – and private accommodation. They may be employed by the local council's hygiene department or work for a commercial company delivering services to a wide variety of clients. Controllers do not need to know about the hazards they will deal with before entering the profession. Thorough training is given so they can identify the particular type of pest causing the problem – and there are many different types of cockroaches, mites, bugs and insects which can cause problems – before deciding on the best course of treatment for the infestation. Treatment can mean using chemical sprays or powders or even fumigating an area, but it is equally about educating the property owner so that their behaviour does not encourage a re-infestation in the future.

Pest controllers therefore use technical skills – for identifying and treating the problem – and interpersonal skills for reassuring the client, telling them what the problem is and how they can help. Going into someone's home in order to deal with an infestation requires a huge amount of diplomacy, especially as the home owner might feel they are being personally blamed for the problem. Handling problems in the commercial sector is even more demanding. Food stores and restaurants can attract many different kinds of pest – a fact which the retailer will not want his customers to know.

Controllers should also be able to work well on their own. They may be under the supervision of an area manager who will allocate work and provide support, but essentially it is a one-person operation – you versus the pest. The job is not for the squeamish – some infestations can be gut churning, but there are also opportunities to leave the fieldwork behind and move into the role of technician where you may be studying the habits of rats, mice and cockroaches in order to develop more effective treatments for the future.

 Highs: Ridding an environment of a pest.

Lows: Working in some very horrible environments.

Funeral director

Strange as it may seem, many people who work with death every day do it because they want to work with people. Not dead people, of course, but with those who are left to grieve. It is easy to see why. Death is a profoundly moving experience and can be tragic and heartbreaking. As a funeral director, you are able to help people through this difficult period, helping them to say farewell to the person who has died and to begin the rest of their lives. Funeral directors effectively stage-manage the funeral – a ritual which marks the end of one person's life and which is as much a celebration of that life as it is a sorrowful occasion.

Funeral directors deal with the entire process of the funeral, taking care of the deceased's body from the point of death through to burial or cremation. They will collect the body from hospital, the mortuary or even from a private address. An embalmer may treat the body so it does not decay and is still presentable to relatives if they wish to pay their last respects. There is a lot of customer centred work to be done – details of the coffin, the service and even the tombstone or memorial must be decided. Eliciting and acting upon this information needs expert people skills to ensure customers explain exactly what they want even though they may be upset and grieving.

On the day itself, it is up to the funeral director to see that all runs smoothly. He or she needs to ensure the vehicles are ready – the hearse and cars for transporting the relatives – that all floral tributes are collected and transported where necessary and that the mourners arrive at the crematorium or churchyard at the right time.

Funeral directors usually receive training on the job, gaining skills and experience with a particular company and gaining more responsibilities as time goes on. The Co-operative Society are well known for their funeral services and run many courses to develop their employees in the job. However, there are also many small funeral directing firms that serve local areas and these will provide you with details of how to apply for work.

 Highs: Helping people at a time of great need.

Lows: Can be depressing – you need to be a particular sort of person to get ongoing job satisfaction from the work.

With
Great
Interest

T urning your hobby into a job can lead you into strange areas of work. You may discover you are able to work offering services to other people who share your interest. Any magazines or information services that you use on a regular basis will prove useful to you, carrying specific vacancies, advertisements from people already offering services and by indicating areas where a new service would be feasible. Alternatively, as a fanatic yourself, you may be well aware of areas for business opportunities serving other interested people. The Internet is a great arena for this kind of work, offering a new medium through which like-minded people can talk to one another about their interests, share information and even trade.

You may not be particularly interested in the areas listed below, but use these examples to help you think about your own passion – whether it is for music, railways or even model making – and try to think of roles you could take in the supply chain from supplier to customer. There is only one danger with turning your hobby into a job and it lies in the fact that hobbies are meant to be separate from daily working life. Turning your interest into part of the daily working routine could result in you losing enthusiasm for the subject.

Philatelist

Stamps have been collectors' items for many years and while the typical collector may be male and in his fifties or sixties, they are by no means limited to this portion of the population. Stamps are collected all over the world and from countries all over the world, with enthusiasts keen to complete collections from particular geographical areas or of certain denominations.

Stanley Gibbons is the UK's largest trading company in stamps but there are many other small privately run firms up and down the country. Stanley Gibbons is large enough to run a showroom in London and serve national and international customers through a mail order service. They even produce publications about stamps. Employees can get to travel all over the world in search of stamps to add to the company's stock. There may be auctions for particular ranges of stamps or deals to be had with suppliers. Naturally the more valuable stamps are those in scant supply – the rarer the stamp, the higher the price one can charge for it – but value can also be affected by the condition of the stamp.

Working for a stamp trader does not simply mean completing mail order services. Traders can design special promotions where enthusiasts sign up to receive stamps forming a particular collection. It is a flexible workplace and one which requires both the enthusiast's knowledge and business skills. At the end of the day, traders must still be able to negotiate a good deal for their stock and put together attractive packages for customers.

There are opportunities to take this market to the Internet – using this as a retail and information outlet that would be more accessible to customers than a single high street location.

Highs: Finding rare stamps and putting together promotions.

Lows: Ensuring you attract sufficient customers to make the business feasible.

Ornithologist

Enthusiastic ornithologists are sometimes known as 'twitchers' – a term which is considered derogatory by some, but taken with pride by others. Jobs available to bird watchers range from straightforward administrative posts at nature reserves or with conservation organizations, all the way through to complex research work in the recording and monitoring of birds and their habitats in the wild.

Fieldwork is often carried out on behalf of conservation societies or as part of wider research centred on universities and biological or environmental pressure groups. It could feature basic atlas and mapping work – recording the sightings of particular species – or may rely on the identification of birds by their song alone. Other evidence might be recorded such as nesting sites or the appearance of droppings. Research is carried out all year round and in all weathers. You can expect to work at any time, day or night and you may need to work in remote or inhospitable locations. There are many opportunities for voluntary work in this area with local groups of the County Conservation Trusts, the British Trust for Conservation as well as through the British Trust for Ornithology itself (British Trust for Ornithology – The Nunnery, Thetford, Norfolk IP24 2PU).

While practical experience will help you find suitable opportunities, some kind of related qualification is likely to net you more interesting and involving work. A levels in biology or other science subjects will help, so too will further and higher degree level qualifications. Adult education courses may also be useful to back up your interest. Whichever educational institution you attend, you may find the establishment has useful links with research groups or is even involved in carrying out its own research programmes.

Highs: Working alongside birds, studying their habits and the effect of the environment upon them.

Lows: Working in all weathers, at all times.

Tarot reader

The tarot is a pack of cards used to predict the fortune of or give spiritual insight into individual people. The deck is divided into different suits – much like a conventional pack of cards – and the way in which the cards are drawn by the enquiring individual is interpreted by the tarot reader. This interpretation is intended to give the enquirer an insight into their own life so that they can make informed decisions about what to do. Guidance may include physical and emotional issues or even career advice.

There are some people who scoff at the idea that a pack of cards can provide any kind of help at all in anyone's life; others, however, feel the tarot does hold special powers and that tarot readers have special gifts. You can learn how to interpret the cards by teaching yourself with a pack from any special interest or mystical shop. Alternatively you may find a reader who is able to offer guidance.

Tarot readers may operate from home, travel to their clients' homes or even open their own consultation rooms. In the case of the latter, location is extremely important. Tarot readers who set up next to shops selling similarly spiritual or mystical oriented goods are likely to attract customers more than those next to the supermarket in the modern shopping mall. As well as learning all the cards, understanding their meanings and how their meanings can be interpreted together, tarot readers must have exceptional people skills. Enquirers are likely to come to you at moments of crisis or with very important questions they would like answered. They will want to analyse everything you say carefully.

Consultations are usually given on a one-to-one basis and may be tape-recorded by the enquirer to take away and listen to later. As time goes by you will find you are able to sense more about the people who visit you through their body language and appearance, but that is not to discredit any mystical gifts you may uncover in yourself as you work with the tarot.

You should be aware that there are some con artists in the field of tarot reading; they may make it difficult for you to gain credibility with some members of the public. Many of the phone line tarot services are nothing more than excuses for companies to make money by keeping callers on premium rate phone lines for long periods of time. In general, however, you will find your customers are already convinced of the positive benefits of tarot reading.

 Highs: Helping people with difficult life decisions.

 Lows: There may be sceptics who you need to win around.

Zoo keeper

Zoos used to have a bad press for incarcerating animals in unsuitable surroundings simply for the fascination of the viewing public. Events such as the *Chimpanzee's Tea Party* had more to do with entertainment than the well-being of the animals involved. This has changed however, with zoos and country parks now taking an active role in the preservation of endangered species from around the world and contributing to the conservation effort. Unsurprisingly, many people who work in this area have zoological and biological qualifications – some may even have trained as veterinary surgeons. However, it is quite common to find zookeepers who have picked up the job simply through personal interest and on the job training.

Through volunteering and working for nothing at your local zoo or wildlife park, you will gain skills in how to look after and manage the wildlife, gaining the trust of the animals themselves and of the full-time staff – the professional keepers – working on site. You may find you slowly gain more responsibilities in the day-to-day management of certain animals or alternatively, you may use your experience as grounds to take an academic course in this area.

Do not expect to be handling the animals from day one – in fact, do not expect to be able to handle the animals at all. These days, keepers prefer to avoid direct contact which could adversely affect the animal, giving it the impression that it is human rather than an actual species and depending less on its natural instincts. At the same time, zoological parks like keepers who will be around for a few years since it means the animals will get to trust those keepers and be happier in their habitat.

Mucking out and food preparation are the most likely tasks you will be given to do. Neither job is particularly glamorous but it is through this kind of routine that problems or changes in animal behaviour can be observed. Keepers now go out of their way to provide as natural a habitat as possible to stimulate each animal and prevent boredom, so you may find yourself able to devise new games for feeding time. Keepers must also deal with the public who visit parks or zoos, dealing with any questions they may have about an animal and ensuring they do not place themselves or the animals in danger.

 Highs: Working with animals.

Lows: You may have to work for a long time before gaining any great responsibilities.

Protester/campaigns organizer

If there is a cause that you firmly believe in, there may be a way you can combine your belief with making money. Charities and pressure groups rely on the work of volunteers to keep their activities going and to raise awareness of their issues throughout the public arena. While these volunteers may not get paid at first, if you stay with an organization for long enough and show your commitment you will be in a prime position to take advantage of any opportunities which do arise.

Work at this level is extremely varied. You may be involved in street collections or promotions, enlisting the support of members of the public towards a particular project or simply raising general awareness. This can be hard work sometimes – some members of the public may not be sympathetic to your viewpoint, might simply not want to know or might not want to donate their hard-earned cash to your cause. On the other hand, the satisfaction of having gained the help or sympathy of even one or two more people can be very rewarding.

If street work does not appeal, some campaigning organizations have very busy back offices that manage and arrange campaigning activities and coordinate the local work with other regional centres around the country. Phone calls and letter writing play an important part in promoting many causes – through press releases, publicity literature, posters or flyers. You may be able to use your imagination to dream up new ways of getting the cause noticed – sponsored events or peaceful demonstrations which can grab news coverage.

Full-time and paid positions are usually advertised both internally and externally, but it is clear that having established a track record with the organization you are likely to be in a good position to apply for full-time work. In spite of the charity status of some pressure groups, careers, pay and benefits can sometimes match the levels of private sector jobs.

Highs: Working for something you believe in.

Lows: There is always a danger of 'burnout' in these jobs.

Chauffeur

If you love cars, why not drive them for a living? True you might not get to be Nigel Mansell but there are plenty of other ways in which to indulge your automobile fascination. People need to be driven around for many different reasons. Celebrities and VIPs are simply too important to drive themselves anywhere. You may find yourself the sole chauffeur of a particular client or working for a chauffeur company used by many different people. You could be driving them to attend important social functions or simply to the shops. Your clients may not always want to attract attention to themselves – a jobbing chauffeur is as likely to find lucrative work ferrying someone around in an unremarkable vehicle as he or she is to be forever dusting down the Bentley.

There are many occasions when general members of the public require car services. Weddings in particular use special chauffeur-driven vehicles – old, new and unique – to add to the important day.

You may find you need to own your own car for this job, but equally, as part of a chauffeur company, it is likely that you will share the vehicles between drivers. You will need a full, clean driving licence and special insurance to cover any accidents that may damage either the vehicle or your passengers. There are obvious financial responsibilities involved with providing your own vehicle – not simply for purchase but for upkeep as well. It will not be sufficient to make sure simply that the vehicle is roadworthy as customers will expect a certain standard of cleanliness both inside and outside the car.

 Highs: Driving around in unusual and attractive vehicles.

Lows: Traffic jams.

Organic shopkeeper

The debate over the merit of organic, non-organic and genetically modified foods has made headlines in recent years. The rise in interest in organic and health foods is unquestionable and today the situation exists where demand for guaranteed organic produce far outstrips supply – growing by almost 50 per cent per year compared with supply which only reaches a 0.3 per cent growth rate. Many supermarkets have realized the potential of the market and are exercising their buying power with organic farmers and produce suppliers, but there is still a place for the small, local organic shop. Indeed such enterprises, with their local focus in terms of the suppliers they use and the other businesses they support in turn, will bring far greater ecological benefits to the local community and the general environment than the supermarkets ever could.

Establishing a shop is, however, a mammoth task. Location is crucial to success – not simply in terms of the customers who pass through the door, but the wider neighbourhood who may be receptive to value added services such as door-to-door box delivery of produce. Aside from the marketing implications of this decision, you must also consider the property you are using, from the layout of the shop to the nature of the lease you are given for the property. Before you start you need to sort out how to finance the operation, who will staff the shop and so on. In general, you cannot expect a new enterprise to start paying its own way for at least three years.

Many shops end up making their money on the 'pills and potions' shelf – a line of goods which includes selling vitamins, mineral supplements, herbal remedies and so on. These goods have a great mark-up price for the retailer that is often used to cover other loss making or break-even product lines. On the other hand, shops can realize profit margins through value added services such as making fresh juice and soup or running box delivery schemes.

It is a good idea to begin by working in a similar shop to see how such a store works. You will find running the shop can be a fairly mundane task – the usual requirements of stocktaking, ordering goods, receiving, pricing and selling goods is similar to other shop work. The difference is that organic produce is more than just another product and can be more than just a lifestyle choice. If you set up the shop carefully it will not only help to promote healthy living among its clientele, it can encourage greater environmental awareness within the locality and even help lessen the impact of twenty-first century living on the planet.

Highs: Creating a business with ecological benefits.

Lows: Setting up and running a shop is a 24-hour, 7 days a week obsession. Do not expect any other life and do not expect the business to start paying you back for at least three years.

Cat sitter

When going away on holiday there are only two options open to the cat lover as to what to do with their beloved moggy. The first of these is to cart it off to a cattery where it will be with many other cats, fed en masse by the cattery staff. However, cats are very territorial animals and are likely to be upset if their routine is broken or worse still, they find themselves in unfamiliar surroundings. The second option is therefore to employ a cat sitter. This person will visit the cat at home while its owner is away, to play with and feed it, ensuring it does not get bored, lonely or very hungry.

Naturally, to be a good cat sitter you need to have an unquestionable love of animals. At the same time, you will need to prove you are trustworthy and responsible. Cat owners may grant you access to their property to look after the cat, but they will not appreciate it if you use their property for other purposes. You will not need any qualifications as such, but you will need to have some good references as to your character and trustworthiness from respected people in the community.

You will also need to have a good level of knowledge about cats – or indeed any other animal you might agree to look after. If the animal starts to behave strangely or show signs of illness, you will need to know what to do and where to take it. Sitters must be prepared to visit the vet and be able to provide the necessary care and attention to nurse it back to health. There may be strict dietary needs for the cat or certain activities that it loves particularly, both of which the cat sitter should follow.

You may find the majority of work in this area comes over the summer months as people go on holiday and it may be possible to look after several cats at the same time. During the rest of the year, there may be opportunities for looking after other domestic animals. Dog-walking companies are quite common in areas where owners spend all day at work or are too old to give their pets the daily exercise they need. You will find contact details of pet-walking companies and other pet sitters in advertisements at the local veterinary surgery. You may find it is easier to start work by helping at established companies, building your experience, rather than starting out on your own from day one.

Highs: Looking after pets.

Lows: Some animals may be unfriendly!

Tree surgeon

If landscape gardening seems a little tame and you want to get higher in the world, tree surgery could be the answer. Instead of a scalpel, the tree surgeon wields clippers and the occasional chain-saw but it is still a precise job for all that. Tree surgeons are used both by public sector organizations and by private clients who experience difficulties with or are concerned about trees on their land. Broken branches may need removing if they present a danger to the public. Alternatively, tall trees can obstruct power lines and endanger buildings. Tree surgeons are frequently called to carry out assessments for house buyers since the roots of some plants can present problems if they dry out the soil around the foundations.

The surgeon must assess the situation presented in each case and carry out any work required. This could mean safely removing large branches without killing off the entire tree, or deciding how to remove a plant completely in the safest and easiest way. Having decided the best course of action, the surgeon then carries out the work. It may be possible to do this from ground level, but more likely, the surgeon will have to scale the tree and work above ground. In this case, safety harnesses must be worn and safety precautions followed.

It is necessary to train to be a tree surgeon before applying for work with a company, or even setting up as a sole trader. As well as learning about horticulture and the life of trees, potential surgeons gain climbing skills and learn the safe use of their equipment. Courses in tree surgery are run at many agricultural colleges but you must still expect to continue learning on the job with your first employer.

Highs: Helping plants grow safely.

Lows: Bad-weather days.

Painting conservator

Removing the rigours of time from an old painting is as much of an art as creating the painting in the first place. The most treasured masterpiece can become foul through neglect or accident – canvases may become torn and layers of dirt can build up reducing the original impact of the painting.

A painting conservator works to reverse this damage and restore the painting to something approaching its original appearance. It is both painstaking and rewarding work, requiring the conservator to apply many different treatments and techniques to the work in order to restore the painting fully. There may be many layers of varnish painted over the original surface that need to be removed. Indeed, this varnish may have to be stripped before the artwork can be retouched or more substantial damage addressed.

It is meticulous work and requires patience and skill as well as a wealth of knowledge of the art world and restoration techniques. The bad news is that training to be a fully qualified painting conservator takes between five and ten years, a period which includes studying art, art history or natural sciences. This is followed by postgraduate training courses in which to learn specific restoration techniques as well as introducing students to the practical side of the work.

In spite of this academic requirement, it is expected that prospective conservators should have a significant amount of practical experience on the job and such work can be found through voluntary work at museums and galleries. Volunteering for this kind of work – usually as a general dogsbody, helping out a qualified conservator – can be done at any time and will give you a good idea of what the work involves before committing such a substantial amount of time to study. Fully qualified conservators may work in studios or for art institutions but it is possible to work on a freelance basis, using your own studio to carry out work on some paintings or travelling to various locations to do work on site when required.

 Highs: Being as close to a painting as the original artist.

Lows: Scraping layers of glue off the back of a canvas with a scalpel can get a bit boring.

Body piercer

Body jewellery has become extremely popular over recent years with metal and stones adorning almost every part of the human body imaginable. For some, body piercing has become something of an obsession – a statement about themselves or an ongoing experiment with their own bodies.

Becoming a body piercer entails taking up an unofficial apprenticeship. In the same way that tattooists pass on their skills to interested individuals or the next generation, qualified piercers also pass their knowledge and techniques to others, ensuring that the individual is aware of and follows all the required health and safety practices connected with the activity. It is extremely rare for an individual to receive training without already having access to a licensed body-piercing studio. Trainee piercers work alongside qualified staff, learning how to prepare for a piercing, using the autoclave to sterilize the piercing needles and to get the necessary consent forms signed by the client. Piercings are carried out in a sterile and safe environment, where the individual being pierced understands what is going to happen and how to look after their body jewellery after the piercing.

Training may simply be a matter of observation at first, but the trainee will eventually take on piercings, all carried out under the watchful eye of their mentor. While the technique is essentially the same for all piercings, the piercer must learn the potential dangers to the circulatory and nervous systems and be able to identify when a piercing is not suitable for a client.

After a year or so, the trainee piercer undergoes a verbal exam covering health and safety procedures to ensure they understand how to pierce safely. Having gained their certificate from the local Department of Health and Consumer Protection, the individual can then pierce on their own.

Highs: Giving people a very special decoration.

Lows: When clients pass out.

**The
Sporty
Kind**

A re you good at games? Are you fit? Are you glued to the TV watching every match, race or contest you can? How about turning that passion into cash? You may not be coordinated enough to make it to Wimbledon and there may not be room for you at Wembley Stadium, but you could make a lucrative career managing and helping to run these and many other venues. You can still get a healthy kick out of your work, running around for the enjoyment of it rather than because your boss has given you too much work to do.

Increased awareness of a healthier lifestyle has paved the way for many job opportunities in the sports sector, such as coaching, training and working out with members of the general public as well as with professional teams. There are also opportunities for those who simply cannot sit still during their working day — people with energy to burn in need of a daily challenge. So do not delay, get under starter's orders and take the plunge.

Rickshaw driver

A physical challenge with a difference – and originally a feature of oriental climes – the rickshaw is a human-powered method of transport, consisting of a cart on two wheels with two long poles that the rickshaw driver pulls. Imagine a single horse and cart, replace the horse with a human and you get the picture. Anything up to four customers can sit in the cart itself and enjoy the ride as the rickshaw driver sweats his or her way through the streets of the town in which he or she operates.

Other human-powered methods of transport are available including four-person taxi bikes enabling one cyclist to pedal passengers around town. The popularity of this and other methods of human-powered transport has increased in the UK. There is now a permanent fleet of pedal-powered taxis in London and rickshaws are also found as novelty transport during local festivals (mainly in cities which do not have extensive hills). Unsurprisingly, rickshaws tend to be more numerous during the summer months since passengers are unlikely to want to ride in quite an exposed position in winter, to say nothing of the feelings of the driver.

Pulling power is not the only qualification needed for this work. It is a people-oriented job which requires both charm and personality from the drivers, allowing them to shine on happily while enduring all weathers, taking orders from customers and pacifying the passing – or more likely, following – motorists. Drivers must be outgoing people since the unique selling-point of the transport is its novelty value. Customers will use human-powered transport as much – and probably more – for its spectacle value as for its ability to get them from A to B.

Advertisements for drivers generally appear in the local press, but it is worth applying directly to any rickshaw company you come across. Obviously, you will also need to have sound knowledge of the area around which you are carting people – it will be more than a little embarrassing if you have to keep asking directions from your passengers.

 Highs: It's a great way to feel part of the city you are working in and to see the nightlife.

Lows: It can be dangerous negotiating traffic and high levels of pollution in built-up areas can make the work unpleasant.

Cycle courier

If you get your kicks on two wheels and have the legs and stamina for biking around all day, cycle couriering could be for you. Couriers can be employed as part of a complete fleet of despatch services ranging from large white vans at the top end of the scale, delivering packages across a substantial area, to motorbikes which flit through the heavily congested streets of cities, delivering smaller parcels. Each method of transport is used for its own qualities and the advantage of a cycle courier is that cyclists can go where no other vehicle can, negotiating traffic jams and taking short cuts impossible in any other method of transport. Admittedly this might not necessarily mean adhering strictly to the highway code at all times, but the cycle courier is employed to get from A to B in the shortest possible time and in one piece.

The work is a great physical challenge and getting a job is usually more of a fitness test than an interview. You will need to supply your own bike and be well versed in maintaining it and ensuring it is operational at all times. Your employer will not be impressed if a delivery goes astray because you spent all day fixing a puncture. You will need to know the local streets and short cuts in detail, be prepared to continue pedalling whatever the weather and be thick-skinned when it comes to other people's appreciation of your road use. Pedestrians and motorists alike are wary of cyclists and couriers have a reputation for being particularly reckless.

Of course, if pedalling is too much like hard work, you could always be a motorbike courier. Even local pizza parlours use moped riders to get their food home-delivered while it is still hot and experience at this level would give you an idea of what it might be like when you are under greater pressure delivering important documents between businesses.

The area of home or door-to-door delivery has made a few

advances recently with the introduction of dial-out services for sushi and other more exotic foods. One entrepreneur has taken a different spin on the theme of using easy transportation to provide a mobile service to customers. If someone goes out in their car and subsequently starts drinking alcohol, they can now phone a special bikeman who will come out to them on his scooter. The scooter is small enough to fit into the boot of most cars so the bikeman can then safely drive the intoxicated client back home in his own car.

Highs: Riding your bike and getting paid for it.

Lows: Traffic, pollution, weather.

Bungee jumper

One of the more bizarre leisure pursuits to have emerged over the last decade has been the practice of throwing oneself from a high-up place attached to something permanent only by a length of industrial strength elastic. While there have been some accidents with the sport, the majority of people who have undertaken the jump have come away feeling euphoric, even using the experience as a life changing event, giving themselves the confidence and belief that they can do anything. It is now rare to attend an outdoor event – festival, fair or pop concert – and not see a crane regularly lifting the next punter to a dizzying height from which to plummet.

Jumps take place all over the world – from famous bridges and impressive natural landscapes as well as from cranes. While each jump takes only seconds, the bungee jump crew are employed for days at a time to set up the equipment and supervise jumpers. It is a people-oriented activity requiring great skills in giving jumpers the reassurance they need before taking the plunge or allowing them to change their minds if they really want to.

Aside from the novelty of the act itself, however, the job can get monotonous. Like other businesses it is necessary to drum up customers, arrange venues for the activity to take place and ensure there is a constant stream of people lining up to jump. There may be special events at which bungee jumping can take place or you may find yourself catering for corporate occasions or even arranging strange requests such as couples getting married just before they jump.

 Highs: An exciting pastime which customers will enjoy immensely, the chance to travel.

 Lows: Possibly monotonous working day – once you have seen one person jump you have seen them all.

Paint-baller

Another reasonably new leisure pursuit is in the field of adventure games. Paint-balling consists of running around a designated area, dressed in combat gear and armed with a gun that shoots paint-balls. It is usually an outdoor pursuit set in woodland or farmland sites given over to armies of paint-ballers at a particular time. In some places, there are paint-balling clubs where members dedicate some of their time every month to paint-balling. At the same time, the sport is also popular for business and corporate entertainment, for birthdays and even for stag parties.

There are some dangers connected to the sport and customer training is always a priority before allowing contestants to set out and shoot one another. Protective clothing should be worn including special facemasks to protect the eyes from a direct hit. For some games, teams of paint-ballers will be set against each other in which case additional supervision may be required to ensure no one gets lost or hurt.

As with bungee jumping crews, day-to-day duties can seem run-of-the-mill but there is always the opportunity to create new challenges for participants and to redesign the area around which the game is played. This could mean landscaping the area or even building hideouts and shelters for players to use.

Laser questing is a similar operation – the paint-ball gun is replaced with a laser gun that shoots a beam of light detected by light-sensitive receptors on each player's body. This time the game is played indoors and once again, there is the opportunity to design exciting environments around which the game can be played – playing with stage sets and atmospheric lighting, dry ice and music.

Highs: Designing and running an exciting and physically demanding game.

Lows: You may find you play the game less as more customers take up the game.

BMX demonstrator

BMX or bicycle motocross is not the most high profile of sports and yet it is possible to make a living out of the activity. Behind every sport is an entire industry making products to support that sport – from running shoes to T-shirts, gym equipment and in the case of BMX, bikes.

BMX demonstrators travel nationally and internationally, raising the awareness of a particular manufacturer's products. They do this by attending exhibitions, competing in races and staging demonstrations. This can mean taking part in a race at a cold and wet track in Central Milton Keynes or using the bikes to jump, do acrobatics and pull stunts at international trade fairs. Product demonstrators must be proficient in their use of the bikes, but they are salespeople as well as show people.

Roles such as these are rarely advertised and even finding out about their existence often means you need to be in the right place at the right time. In BMX, there is a healthy national scene of meetings and races where riders compete for national titles. At such meetings, there can be representatives from the manufacturing companies or equipment distributors who are keen to find successful riders who will boost the profile of their equipment. The same will be true of other sports and if you cannot find those people, you can always contact the manufacturers directly and find out how they promote their products.

Even sales people in this area of work find themselves showered with free state-of-the-art equipment, the idea being that they will promote that particular brand in preference to others. But while the chance to play around on your bike or with other kinds of sports equipment may seem like a dream, the other side of the job is that such work usually has a sales or promotional target to reach. This is extremely important if such staff are to keep hold of their jobs.

Highs: Play all day and get top-range equipment.

Lows: There is still an amount of bureaucracy and office work between trips.

Diver

Professional divers work in various parts of industry. Diving can be simply a leisure pursuit and many trainers find themselves work in holiday resorts across the world, teaching people to dive or accompanying them on trips to see the wonders of the deep. At the same time, divers are used by other seabound industries. The oil industry for example uses divers to carry out undersea rig inspections and maintenance work. Divers may also find work in salvage operations where goods need to be retrieved from the sea. They may even be used in an investigative capacity to discover clues as to why a vessel sank.

Learning to dive is a demanding and rewarding exercise, but can be expensive. Training courses for beginners are recognized by the Professional Association of Diving Instructors (PADI) or the British Sub-Aqua Club (tel: 0151 350 6200) who can also put you in touch with your nearest diving school. The PADI Open Water course is designed for beginners, qualifying them for dives of up to 18 metres. It costs around £230 and lasts for five days. Other courses give divers qualifications in areas such as ocean diving, wreck diving and leading a dive. While you can hire equipment, if you are taking the activity seriously you will need to buy your own wet suit, air tanks and other equipment, all of which can take the cost into thousands of pounds.

Once trained, there are no easy ways to get work as a professional diver. In general, you should get in touch with some of the clients listed above and offer your services. Alternatively, the diving schools themselves may have useful employment contacts or could employ you to pass on your skills.

Highs: See things other people never will.

 Lows: Some danger is involved with every dive.

Sports/aerobics instructor

Why not earn money while keeping fit? In today's world, more and more people are health conscious and concerned that while their lifestyle may be enjoyable it might not be too healthy. As a result, a weekly visit to the local gym provides the chance to get back in trim and to feel good before submitting to the rigours and temptations of another week.

Aerobics is only one method of keeping fit. Communal sports classes can also include kickboxing or yoga, or even focus on specific parts of the body such as the legs or abdominal muscles. If you are going to lead a class in this kind of activity you need to be extremely confident in what you are going to do, obviously super-fit – you need to talk and demonstrate at the same time – and very good with people. Very often, there will be stragglers or newcomers to the class who will need all the encouragement you can give them.

Another trend in this area is the use of the personal coach. This is someone who will work on physical activities on a one-to-one basis with clients. Clients may have a specific need or something to achieve from their exercise – building stamina or upper body strength for example, and you will need to design a training regime tailored to those needs. Again, people skills are extremely important here, as you will need to explain how to do the exercises properly, what the exercises are designed to do and offer loads of encouragement.

There are many options for entering this area of work and becoming an instructor. Many college courses cover physical education and will also give you the human biology knowledge required. At the same time, your local gym may also have some training opportunities, even running an NVQ scheme in this area. Whichever path you choose, your first port of call should be the local sports centre.

Highs: Physical exercise produces body chemicals that make you happy!

Lows: You may find yourself permanently tired out.

Stadium groundsperson

There is more to looking after a sports pitch than watering and cutting it every so often. Growing grass for sports purposes has turned into an exact science. The truly proficient groundsman needs to understand the effects of rainfall, of sunshine and of atmospheric conditions on the turf. This has become all the more important as venues have increased the number of fixtures they have each season. Fresh demands are also made of the pitch's turf as sports arenas play host to non-sporting events such as rock concerts and rallies. Some venues have even started to use movable turf in order to enable other events to take place without damaging the pitch. Synthetic grass is not popular among footballers, so the current trend is to create a 'live' pitch on a series of pallets that can then be moved when the occasion demands. These pallets present their own problems in terms of ensuring sufficient drainage for healthy turf. Even building technology has created new challenges for turf specialists with removable roofs offering the choice of protecting the pitch from the elements.

While this change in the management of pitches has led to the introduction of some very specialist courses in turf technology, the simplest way into grounds work is through voluntary work. You may not be paid and the work could be extremely mundane for a while, but by being there, you will learn how to look after the turf all year round. In addition, some colleges will only accept students who have a proven interest in this area and already have practical experience of looking after a pitch.

Grounds people are used worldwide. In the USA there are even groundsman agencies that assign highly experienced staff to well-known venues across the country – golf courses and luxury hotel grounds – as well as to football and baseball pitches. The work itself is more painstaking than demanding. There may be some heavy manual work to be done but it is more about knowing how to treat a pitch or field. Ground staff must know when to tend the turf and how to repair the damage inflicted on it during use. This can be quite a high pressure job in some cases since events such as Wimbledon or major football matches will be televised and hold national and international significance. Any suggestion that the ground is not in tip-top condition will not only look bad for the venue but could cause problems for the image of the game across the world.

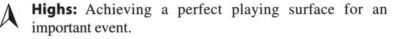 **Highs:** Achieving a perfect playing surface for an important event.

 Lows: Irregular hours.

Demolition person

It may seem to be a little backwards but in order to be a decon-struction expert one must first gain qualifications with the Construction Industry Training Board (tel: 01553 776677). On the other hand, this makes perfect sense: taking down a building safely can only be done with an understanding of how construction works – how buildings fit together. Attacking a random wall in a block of flats with a sledgehammer is unlikely to have the desired effect.

Demolition operatives start their careers with a demolition company and undergo training on the job. This training covers safety on site, accident prevention and personal safety, the control of asbestos and lead and even the control of noise pollution. The trainee will also learn how to prevent fires occurring and how to react if they do. At this stage, the trainee will have nothing to do with any machinery and will certainly not be given a load of explosives to set and detonate. These are specialist areas that require a good deal of on-site experience and additional training.

Before demolition takes place, the workers need to assess the materials which will be produced by the deconstruction and decide how these materials will be handled. Measures are taken to control the dust created during the demolition process and hazardous materials will require special packing. Demolition workers could find themselves dealing with relatively low hazards in areas such as urban renewal, but other contracts might involve cleaning up chemicals and dealing with other environmentally unfriendly waste products.

Plant such as specially equipped JCBs and diggers is often used to cut through reinforced concrete or iron supports and oper-ating this kind of equipment requires a good deal of training. Blowing up a building is a strategic job. Explosive experts care-fully set the right charges at certain locations in a building, even removing supporting walls to ensure the building comes down first time. The explosion must be planned carefully so that the building comes down in the right area – there could be other buildings nearby which it would be a good idea to leave standing at the end of the day. There may also be electricity power lines or sewers underneath the building that must not be damaged by the blast.

However the building is brought down, safety is always the prime consideration for both the individuals working on site and for the general public. The demolition operative must therefore be able to work responsibly within a team and be able to take the initiative in order to reduce hazards as the demolition progresses.

Highs: Regenerating land for reuse.

Lows: Hard manual labour in order to gain responsibilities.

Visit Kogan Page on-line

Comprehensive information on
Kogan Page titles

Features include

- complete catalogue listings,
  including book reviews and
  descriptions

- on-line discounts on a variety
  of titles

- special monthly promotions

- information and discounts on
  NEW titles and BESTSELLING titles

- a secure shopping basket facility
  for on-line ordering

- infoZones, with links and
  information on specific areas of
  interest

PLUS everything you need to know
about KOGAN PAGE

http://www.kogan-page.co.uk